THE WEIRDEST ANIMALS OF THE WORLD
Book for Kids

WONDERFUL WORLD OF ANIMALS BOOK 2

JACK LEWIS

The Weirdest Animals of the World Book for Kids
Wonderful World of Animals Book 2
Copyright © 2021 by Starry Dreamer Publishing

For information contact:
Starry Dreamer Publishing LLC
1603 Capitol Ave.
Suite 310 A377
Cheyenne, Wyoming 82001
starrydreamerpub@gmail.com

Written by Jack Lewis
Photo Credits: All images contained herein are used under license from Shutterstock.com (See Index for complete list)
Front Cover Photo Credits:
V_E, Reptiles4all, Marie Dirgova, Yakov Oskanov/Shutterstock
Back Cover Photo Credits:
Podolnaya Elena, Feathercollector, Khlungcenter/Shutterstock

ISBN: 978-1-952328-94-7 (Hardcover) 978-1-952328-65-7 (Paperback)
978-1-952328-67-1 (Ebook)
Library of Congress Cataloging-in-Publication Data is available
10 9 8 7 6 5 4 3 2 1
First Edition: Jan 2022

STARRY DREAMER PUBLISHING

ECHIDNA
Australia, Indonesia, and Papa New Guinea

Echidnas are spiky mammals that look like a cross between a porcupine and an anteater. Even though they are mammals, they lay eggs instead of giving live birth. Each quill on the echidna has its own muscle that enables the animal to control the spine's direction and movement.

RED-LIPPED BATFISH

Pacific Ocean near the Galápagos Islands

WEIRD FACT:

THE RED-LIPPED BATFISH CAN EXTEND THEIR FLESHY DORSAL FIN AND USE IT AS A LURE TO ATTRACT PREY!

This is one peculiar fish! Instead of swimming, it uses its fins as legs and walks along the sandy bottom of reefs or ocean floors. And let's not forget to mention those bright-red pouty lips!

What are the Galápagos Islands?

The Galápagos Islands are a chain of islands in the Pacific Ocean by South America. The Galápagos Islands comprise thirteen larger islands and several smaller ones, and they are about 600 miles (966 km) off the coast of Ecuador. Over many years, repeated volcanic eruptions helped form the mountainous landscapes of the islands.

Why are the Galápagos Islands so unique?

The Galápagos Islands are famous for their vast array of animal and plant species. Scientists have been studying these islands and their creatures for almost 200 years. Many species that live here are not found anywhere else in the world! This is because their environment is unique. The islands are isolated, and they have an unusual mix of temperate and tropical climates. Over time, this environment has contributed to a very diverse and beautiful assortment of plant and animal life.

Here are just a few of the amazing animals that can be found only on the Galápagos Islands:

- Galápagos penguins
- Flightless cormorants
- Marine iguanas
- Giant Galápagos tortoises
- Galápagos land iguanas
- Frigatebirds
- Darwin's finches
- Blue-footed boobies
- Sally Lightfoot crabs

TUFTED DEER
East Asia

Tufted deer are no ordinary deer! They are mainly found in China and Tibet, although their numbers in the wild are in decline. With their black or brown tufts of hair on their head and large canine teeth, these deer are unmistakably strange in appearance.

LEAFY SEA DRAGON
Coastal Waters of Australia

WEIRD FACT:

ALTHOUGH THE FEMALE SEA DRAGON LAYS THE EGGS, THE MALE WILL CARRY THEM NEAR HIS TAIL UNTIL THEY HATCH!

Although they may not look like it, leafy sea dragons are fish, but they are poor swimmers. They rely on their leafy appendages to blend in and hide with kelp and seaweed.

RED-EYED TREE FROG
Central and South America

WEIRD FACT:

RED-EYED TREE FROGS WILL RETRACT THEIR EYES INTO THEIR BODY TO HELP THEM SWALLOW AND PUSH FOOD DOWN THEIR THROATS!

Even though they are not poisonous, these little frogs rely on their beautiful colors to warn predators. An animal brightly colored is often poisonous or venomous, and these frogs hope that the predator will think they are too.

PEACOCK MANTIS SHRIMP
Pacific and Indian Oceans

WEIRD FACT:

BASED UPON THE DESIGN OF THIS AMAZING SHRIMP'S SHELL, SCIENTISTS HAVE CREATED A NEW TYPE OF MATERIAL THAT CAN BE USED IN AIRCRAFT PANELS AND BODY ARMOR!

These beautiful but brutal sea creatures have deadly appendages they use as clubs. They can strike prey at 50 miles per hour and punch so hard it smashes shells and can split fingers to the bone.

AYE-AYE
Madagascar

Aye-ayes will tap on branches and listen for larvae or moving insects inside. They puncture the wood with their sharp teeth and scoop out the prey with their long fingers if they hear movement.

GIANT ISOPOD
Oceans Across the World

WEIRD FACT:

GIANT ISOPODS CAN GO A LONG TIME WITHOUT EATING. FOR EXAMPLE, ONE ISOPOD IN A JAPANESE AQUARIUM WENT FIVE YEARS WITHOUT EATING A SINGLE BITE!

Like tiny pill bugs you might find in the garden, the giant isopod will curl itself up into a ball when it feels threatened. The isopod's tough shell acts as armor plating to protect it from predators.

11

FOSSA
Madagascar

Although they're related to the mongoose, the strange-looking fossa looks like a cross between cats and dogs. They love to hunt and feed on another famous Madagascar animal, lemurs.

SHOEBILL
Africa

WEIRD FACT:

WITH ITS HUGE, RAZOR-SHARP BEAK, THE SHOEBILL CAN HUNT LARGE PREY, EVEN BABY CROCODILES!

The shoebill is a tall, African bird with a massive bill. They can stand motionless in water for long periods while waiting for prey. They are some of the slowest flying birds and can only fly shorter distances.

BLUE DRAGON
Atlantic, Pacific, and Indian Oceans

WEIRD FACT:

ALTHOUGH IT MAY LOOK INNOCENT, THE BLUE DRAGON IS VENOMOUS AND PACKS A DEADLY STING FOR ANYONE WHO DARES TOUCH ITS BODY!

This interesting species also goes by the name "blue sea slug." They float upside down by using the surface tension of the water to stay up near the surface of the water, then ocean currents and winds can carry them along.

HONDURAN WHITE BAT
Central America

WEIRD FACT:

THESE BATS CONSTRUCT LITTLE WATERPROOF TENTS OUT OF LEAVES TO STAY DRY FROM RAIN AND HIDE FROM PREDATORS!

Found deep in the rainforests of Central America, these white bats feed almost exclusively on figs but can consume other fruits too. Their bizarre "nose-leaf" is thought to assist them with their echolocation calls.

15

HUMMINGBIRD HAWK-MOTH

Across the World

WEIRD FACT:

THE HUMMINGBIRD MOTH'S COILED TONGUE MEASURES ABOUT DOUBLE THE LENGTH OF ITS BODY!

The hummingbird hawk-moth resembles a weird cross between a bird and a bug! This speedy moth beats its wings up to 70 times a second and can fly as fast as 12 miles per hour.

ASIAN GIANT SOFTSHELL TURTLE
Southeast Asia

WEIRD FACT:

THESE FRESHWATER TURTLES CAN LIVE TO BE OVER 100 YEARS OLD!

Asian giant softshell turtles spend much of their life buried and motionless, with only their mouth and eyes protruding from the sand. Twice a day, they surface to catch prey and eat.

SNUB-NOSED MONKEY
China

Unfortunately, these unique monkeys are an endangered species. Due to deforestation and poaching, their numbers in the wild are rapidly decreasing. They will spend most of their lives in the trees where they like to eat bamboo buds, tree needles, fruits, and leaves.

WARTY FROGFISH
Indo-West Pacific Ocean

WEIRD FACT:
THESE FISH CAN OPEN THEIR BIG MOUTHS SO WIDE THEY CAN SWALLOW PREY NEARLY AS LARGE AS THEMSELVES!

These colorful marine fish can be found among corals and sponges in shallow reefs. They have the amazing ability to change their colors and patterns to blend into their surroundings.

AARDVARK
Africa

Aardvarks may look weird, but they are amazing diggers with a great sense of hearing and smell. They love ants and termites and will eat up to 50,000 a night. An aardvark usually closes its nostrils while eating to prevent insects from entering its nose.

GOLDEN TORTOISE BEETLE
North America

WEIRD FACT:

BABY BEETLES, OR "LARVAE," USE THEIR POOP TO MAKE A SHIELD THAT HELPS PROTECT THEM FROM SMALL PREDATORS!

Also known as "goldbugs," these interesting insects are considered pests by many gardeners. They feed on plant foliage and especially like sweet potato plants.

LONG-WATTLED UMBRELLABIRD
East Asia

Umbrella birds have a distinctive crest on top of their head, resembling an umbrella. Male umbrella birds will fan their crests out and call out to the females during mating season.

WEIRD FACT:

A MALE UMBRELLABIRD'S LONG WATTLE CAN GROW UP TO OVER A FOOT IN LENGTH!

DUGONG
Pacific and Indian Oceans

Dugongs are gentle sea mammals related to manatees. Using their flexible upper lips, they'll snatch up entire plants from the seafloor, shake them with their head to clean off the sand, and then swallow their food.

LEAF-TAILED GECKO
Madagascar

WEIRD FACT:

THESE GECKOS HAVE NO EYELIDS, SO THEY WIPE THEIR EYES WITH THEIR LONG, MOBILE TONGUES!

The name of this little gecko accurately describes its strange appearance. They are experts at avoiding predators through their camouflage, mimicry, and the ability to shed their tails.

OKAPI
Africa

These shy woodland creatures look like a cross between a zebra and a horse, but they are closely related to giraffes. For years Europeans living in Africa called them "the African unicorn."

SEA LAMPREY

Atlantic Ocean, Europe, and North America

WEIRD FACT:

SINCE THE MIDDLE AGES, THE LAMPREY FISH HAS BEEN CONSIDERED A DELICACY IN FRANCE!

Sea lampreys, also known as "vampire fish," will latch on to other fish with their spiky teeth and suck their blood to feed. Although they look like eels, they are not related to them. They spend part of their lives in freshwater and part of their lives in saltwater.

27

SAIGA ANTELOPE
Russia and Kazakhstan

The Saiga antelope are a critically endangered species that once inhabited vast areas of Europe and Asia. Due to uncontrolled hunting and demand for their horns, the Saiga population has fallen dramatically. With their large, odd snouts, these antelope are unforgettable!

WEIRD FACT:

THIS ANTELOPE'S LARGE NOSE HELPS COOL THE ANIMAL'S BLOOD IN SUMMER AND HEATS THE FRIGID AIR THEY BREATHE IN WINTER!

MATA MATA
South America

WEIRD FACT:
THE MATA MATA SWALLOWS FISH WHOLE BECAUSE THEY CANNOT CHEW THEIR FOOD!

Have you ever seen a turtle as weird as this one? Amazon rainforests or wetlands are where you'll find this oddly shaped reptile. They like to stay in shallow waters where they can hide and poke their nose out to breathe.

OCEAN SUNFISH
Oceans Across the World

WEIRD FACT:

AN OCEAN SUNFISH CANNOT CLOSE ITS MOUTH!

The gigantic ocean sunfish is one of the heaviest bony fish in the world. Large specimens can measure 14 feet high, 10 feet across, and weigh over 5,000 pounds!

JABIRU
Central and South America

This enormous stork is the tallest flying bird found in Central and South America. They stand five feet tall and have massive wingspans that can measure over nine feet wide.

STICK INSECT
Worldwide

WEIRD FACT:
STICK INSECTS ARE AMONG THE WORLD'S LARGEST INSECTS, WITH SOME SPECIMENS MEASURING OVER 2 FEET IN LENGTH!

There are over 3,000 stick insect species across the world. These bizarre insects are masters of disguise and resemble twigs or plants. They will even mimic the motion of twigs swaying in the wind to throw off predators.

GHARIAL
India and Nepal

WEIRD FACT:

GHARIALS HAVE SPECIAL SENSORS IN THEIR SNOUTS THAT ALLOW THEM TO DETECT VIBRATIONS IN THE WATER AND TARGET THEIR PREY!

These are some creepy crocodiles! Sadly, they are critically endangered species due to hunting and habitat destruction. The gharial's population has decreased by 98% since the 1940s.

MEXICAN MOLE LIZARD
North and Central America

WEIRD FACT:
THEY CAN BREAK OFF THEIR TAIL TO ESCAPE A PREDATOR, BUT IT WILL NOT GROW BACK!

This burrowing reptile species spends most of its life underground. Due to their appearance, they are sometimes mistaken for snakes, but these critters are harmless. They have no back legs, but they use their front legs with claws to dig into the soil.

HAIRY FROG FISH
Oceans Across the World

The hairy frogfish is a bizarre creature. It can change its color to blend in with the coral and seaweed it hides in. It has an extra-long spine on its dorsal fin that waves around to look like a worm and attract prey to eat.

MALAYAN TAPIR
Asia

WEIRD FACT:

WHEN DIVING, TAPIRS USE THEIR LONG, FLEXIBLE NOSE AS A SNORKEL, HELPING THEM BREATHE UNDERWATER!

A Tapir will use its elongated nose to grasp fruits and vegetation and bring the food to its mouth to eat. As you can imagine, with a nose like that, tapirs also have a highly developed sense of smell.

LOWLAND STREAKED TENREC
Madagascar

WEIRD FACT:

THESE TENRECS LOVE TO EAT EARTHWORMS. THEY WILL STOMP THEIR FEET TO GET THE WORMS MOVING SO THEY CAN FIND THEM EASILY!

Strangely enough, the lowland streaked tenrec can communicate using their quills. They will rub them together to make a sound too high to be perceived by human ears, but other animals can hear it.

WHITEMARGIN STARGAZER
Indo-Pacific Ocean

WEIRD FACT:

THIS FISH HAS A HAIRY TONGUE IT WAVES AROUND TO ATTRACT LITTLE FISH, THEN SUCKS THEM IN WHOLE WHEN THEY GET TOO CLOSE!

You do not want to mess with these creepy-looking fish. They have poisoned spines and electric organs that can give quite a shock!

MARKHOR
Central Asia

WEIRD FACT:

THE MARKHOR CAN JUMP OVER 8 FEET HIGH!

This odd goat has some highly unusual, swirly horns. They are the national animal of Pakistan and are known there as the "screw-horned goat." There are less than 2,500 of these goats left in the wild.

TREE PANGOLINS
Africa

WEIRD FACT:

WHEN A TREE PANGOLIN IS ROLLED TIGHTLY IN A BALL, IT IS ALMOST IMPOSSIBLE FOR A PERSON TO UNROLL THEM!

These unusual, armored critters roll into a ball for protection if they feel in danger. Pangolins love to eat ants, and they have special muscles to close their ear openings and nostrils to keep them from crawling in when feeding.

41

BILBY
Australia

Bilbies may look odd, but they sure are cute too! Although bilbies have kangaroo-like hind legs, they do not hop. They gallop like a horse when moving fast. Bilbies are amazing diggers and can dig a hole deep enough to hide in just three minutes.

MANED WOLF
South America

WEIRD FACT:
THE MANED WOLF IS NEITHER A FOX, WOLF, NOR DOG; IT IS THE ONLY SPECIES IN ITS GENUS!

Long-legged and reddish, this animal looks like a fox on stilts. The maned wolf is South America's largest native canine and is also known as the "skunk wolf" due to the strong smell of its territorial markings.

LILAC-BREASTED ROLLER

Africa

This is one beautiful, multi-colored bird! They're known for amazing aerial acrobatic displays of swooping, diving and rolling side-to-side during courtship.

WEIRD FACT:

THESE CLEVER BIRDS WILL TAKE ADVANTAGE OF BRUSH FIRES. AS INSECTS AND SMALL ANIMALS FLEE THE FLAMES, THE LILAC-BREASTED ROLLER WILL SWOOP IN FOR EASY HUNTING!

STAR-NOSED MOLE
North America

WEIRD FACT:

THE TENTACLES ON THE MOLE'S NOSE MOVE EXTREMELY QUICKLY AND CAN TOUCH UP TO 12 OBJECTS PER SECOND!

The star-nosed mole is one fascinating animal! They use their amazing tentacled nose to locate prey. The Guinness Book of World Records lists this species among the fastest hunters in the world.

HORSESHOE CRAB
Atlantic Ocean

WEIRD FACT:

THE BLUE-COLORED BLOOD OF HORSESHOE CRABS IS USED TO HELP CREATE VACCINES AND MEDICATIONS!

Despite its name, the horseshoe crab is more closely related to scorpions and spiders than to crabs. Their mouths are in the center of their legs, and they have ten eyes!

47

BUFF-TIP MOTH
Europe and Asia

WEIRD FACT:
THE BUFF-TIP CATERPILLARS' YELLOW, ORANGE AND BLACK COLORING LET PREDATORS KNOW THAT THEY ARE POISONOUS IF EATEN!

Masters of disguise, these moths blend in perfectly with their surroundings and can look just like the twig of a birch tree. They begin their life as brightly colored caterpillars and dig themselves into the ground over winter, only to emerge in spring as a moth.

THORNY DEVIL
Australia

These spiky lizards are covered entirely with hard, thorny scales. They eat thousands of ants a day and can live to be 20 years old.

BLOTCHED FANTAIL RAY
Indo-West Pacific Region

It's a good thing this large stingray is non-aggressive because it can whip its sharp venomous spine with deadly accuracy if it feels threatened. The blotched fantail ray prefers coral reefs and sandy bottoms to feed on crabs, shrimp, and bottom fish.

AXOLOTL
Mexico

WEIRD FACT:

AXOLOTLS HAVE GILLS TO BREATHE UNDERWATER AND LUNGS TO BREATHE THE AIR ABOVE THE WATER'S SURFACE!

These unique salamanders may live their entire lives in the water. They can live up to 15 years surviving on a diet of worms, insect larvae, small fish, and mollusks.

TAMANDUA
South America

This long-snouted anteater can be found in South America. This species is also known as the "Stinker of the Forest" due to the strong, foul scent it gives off. The smelly odor is about four times stronger than a skunk's stink.

GLASS FROG
Central and South America

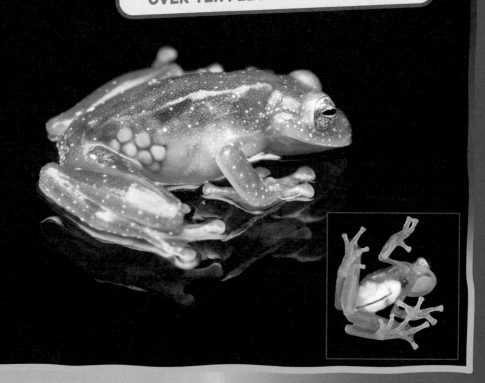

These fascinating frogs have transparent bellies, revealing all their internal organs. Their translucent skin makes them less noticeable and gives them a bit of camouflage to hide from birds.

ARMADILLO
North, Central, and South America

The word armadillo means "little armored one" in Spanish. The armor on these mammals protects them from predators and keeps them insulated against extreme temperatures.

ALLIGATOR GAR
North and Central America

WEIRD FACT:

ALLIGATOR GAR EGGS ARE HIGHLY POISONOUS TO HUMANS AND OTHER ANIMALS IF EATEN!

With its razor-sharp teeth and wide crocodilian head, it's easy to see how this mega fish got its name. It can grow up to 10 feet in length and weigh as much as 350 pounds.

SPINY BUSH VIPER

Africa

These strange venomous vipers like to hunt their prey in the trees. Their spiky scales give them camouflage in the foliage. They use their tails to hang from the branches while waiting to ambush their prey.

WEIRD FACT:

THERE IS NO ANTIDOTE TO THE
SPINY BUSH VIPER'S VENOM!

SRI LANKA FROGMOUTH

Sri Lanka and India

WEIRD FACT:

WHEN THESE BIRDS GET STARTLED, THEY MOVE THEIR LARGE HEAD TO POINT THEIR BILL UPWARDS AND STAY VERY STILL, SO THEY RESEMBLE A TREE BRANCH!

Frogmouth birds earned their name from their wide beaks and goofy appearance. They are nocturnal like owls and are mostly active at night.

DAISY PARROTFISH
Pacific and Indian Ocean

WEIRD FACT:

BEFORE FALLING ASLEEP, THE DAISY PARROTFISH SECRETES MUCUS TO SURROUND ITSELF IN A SLIMY COCOON!

Believe it or not, the colorful daisy parrotfish can change its gender throughout its lifetime. Males can become females and vice versa depending on the social and environmental cues which trigger the changes.

BABIRUSA
Indonesia

The huge "tusks" found on male babirusas are overgrown canine teeth that have broken through the skin. This animal is sometimes called the "deer-pig" because of its similar appearance to swine and how its teeth resemble the antlers of a deer.

JAPANESE SPIDER CRAB
Pacific Ocean

WEIRD FACT:

BABY JAPANESE SPIDER CRABS WILL DECORATE THEIR SHELLS WITH SEA ANEMONES OR SPONGES FOR CAMOUFLAGE!

These gigantic crabs are the largest crustaceans on earth and can measure over 12 feet from claw to claw. They are not only huge, but they can also live up to 100 years!

SEA PEN
Oceans Across the World

WEIRD FACT:
MOST SEA PENS WILL GLOW OR "LUMINESCE" WHEN TOUCHED!

These odd marine invertebrates look a lot like an old-fashioned quill pen. They can deflate or expand by sucking in water into their body, and they feed on plankton or tiny pieces of dead plants or animals.

NAKED MOLE-RAT
Africa

The naked mole-rat is one weird animal! This rodent is neither a rat nor a mole. It is almost blind and spends much of its life as part of a colony underground. It can live nearly 30 years, making it one of the longest living rodents in the world.

INDEX

Enjoy these other great books by JACK LEWIS:

Never Bring a Zebracorn to School

Joy to the World: The Best Christmas Gift Ever

Wonderful World of Animals Series

Take a trip around the world to find the wildest, weirdest, and most adorable animals on the planet!

The Cutest Animals of the World

The Weirdest Animals of the World

The Most Dangerous Animals in the World

Today I Found... Series

Magical children's stories of friendship and the power of imagination!

Today I Found a Unicorn

Today I Found a Mermaid

Today I Found an Elf

Fun with Family Series

A wonderful way to celebrate each special person in our families!

I Love My Mommy

Made in the USA
Columbia, SC
15 November 2023

26386469R00038